THE ART OF SPOONING

The Art of Spooning
A Cuddler's Handbook

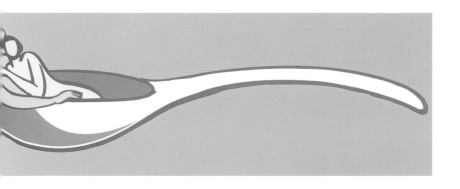

by Jim Grace and Lisa Goldblatt Grace

Illustrated by Alison Seiffer

RUNNING PRESS
PHILADELPHIA · LONDON

ACKNOWLEDGEMENTS

We'd like to gratefully thank all the friends and family who encouraged us, inspired us, and humored us as we obsessed about spooning; especially, the Goldblatts and the Graces, Dave and Suzanne (without whom this book would only have been a twinkle in Jimmy's eye), Robin, Brett and Julie, Joanna, Brangie (who invented the "X"), Tim, the Quinns, Rich, John, Amy and Mike (who were even willing to try out new spoons on our floor), Deb and Eric, the Lewises (who gave Lisa "Theodore the Bear," her first spoon), and all the other people from whom Jim shamelessly solicited spooning ideas. Special thanks to Running Press and our editor, Amy Janke, who believed that spooning should be a household word.

Text © 1998 by Jim Grace
and Lisa Goldblatt Grace
Illustrations © 1998 by Alison Seiffer

All rights reserved under the Pan-American
and International Copyright Conventions

Printed in China

This book may not be reproduced in whole or in part, in any form or
by any means, electronic or mechanical, including photocopying,
recording, or by any information storage and retrieval system now known
or hereafter invented, without written permission from the publisher.

9   8   7   6
Digit on the right indicates the number of this printing

Library of Congress Cataloging-in-Publication Number 97-66837

ISBN 0-7624-0270-9

Designed by Frances J. Soo Ping Chow
Edited by Elizabeth Amy Janke
Typography: Nofret

This book may be ordered by mail from the publisher.
Please include $2.50 for postage and handling.
But try your bookstore first!

Running Press Book Publishers
125 South Twenty-second Street
Philadelphia, Pennsylvania 19103-4399

Contents

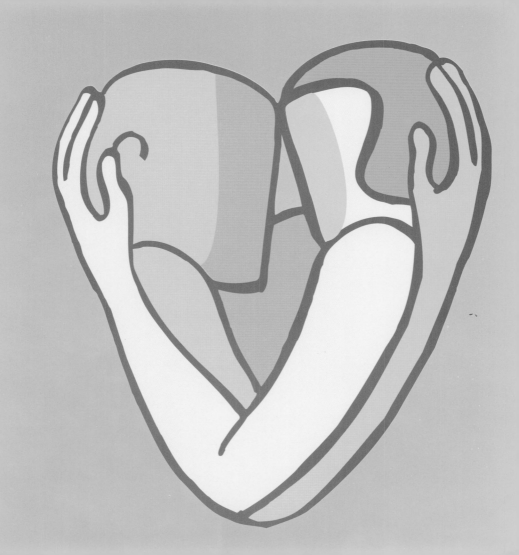

The Making of a Spooner

"To accomplish great spoons, we must not only act, but also dream, not only plan, but also believe."

A GREAT SPOONING WOMAN IN HISTORY

So you're asking yourself, how can we write an entire book about spooning? Here's our story, plain and simple. To be honest, it all began with Lisa. Lisa's love affair with spooning began with a favorite teddy bear named Theodore. Jim had no bear. Never spooned. Hadn't heard of it and by all appearances wasn't interested. Then Jim and Lisa met, fell in love, and, well, you can guess the rest. Inevitably, the spooning issue reared its ugly head.

Would Lisa consent to staying on her own side? Would Jim convert to the philosophy of spooning? The answer became clear right away. Lisa found that teaching Jim to spoon was a gift that kept on giving. After all, Theodore was a good first partner, but she needed to move on. And let's be honest: Jim had no choice. Despite himself, he became enamored with spooning. As it is always with converts, he developed into the most zeal-ous spooner. Really, it seemed he was a natural or . . . perhaps a little obsessed.

This book was born from two sources. First, there was Jim's obsession. "Shouldn't we tell the world about spooning?" he'd ask. "Do you think we could get on Oprah?" Jim became focused on making spooning a household word. He turned into a proselytizing fool. We'd be at parties and there would be Jim—pen in hand—taking notes on the reported spooning habits of our friends like a war correspondent turned pop anthropologist.

Second, Lisa is a social worker. She felt a responsibility to pass on anything that increases the general quality of life and doesn't require a block grant. For Lisa, this book was an opportunity to share with the public one of life's simple pleasures: the spoon. She might even use this as her platform when she runs for secretary of health and human services.

Hence, an entire book about spooning. Spoon on.

A Philosophy of Spooning

"To Spoon or not to Spoon: That is the question."
ELIZABETHAN PLAYWRIGHT AND CLOSET SPOONER

THE DEFINITION OF SPOONING

SPOON (SPÜN) N. 1. A UTENSIL FOR USE IN EATING AND COOKING TO STIR, MEASURE, LADLE, ETC., CONSISTING OF A SMALL SHALLOW BOWL WITH A HANDLE. 2. A SPOONFUL. 3. SOMETHING RESEMBLING A SPOON IN SHAPE (USU. A METAL FISHING LURE) 4. BORN WITH A SILVER SPOON IN ONE'S MOUTH. V. 1. TO TAKE UP AND USU. TRANSFER IN A SPOON. 2. TO PROPEL (A BALL) BY A WEAK LIFTING STROKE. 3. (V; SLANG) TO SHOW AFFECTION OR LOVE, ESP. IN AN OPENLY SENTIMENTAL MANNER.

Though it seems that sleeping, napping, and sex have received all the good press lately for in-the-bed activities, there's another one of life's simple pleasures two can pursue in this venue: spooning.

What is spooning, you may wonder? Spooning is two bodies curling around each other, fitting perfectly into each other's nooks and other comfortable places. The embodiment of the power of touch, the spoon provides a physical and emotional connection unlike any other. It's magical,

WHAT'S A NOOK?
For those of you who've never encountered this word in the context of spooning, we think you're gonna love it. Picture your partner's body in flannel pajamas. Now, think of all the warm, comfortable places you'd like to nestle into, the place you'd like to rest your weary head at the end of a long day. The technical term for this comfy place is a nook. We challenge you to use this word in a sentence within the next twenty-four hours.

in its own sort of way. Spooning is about limbs and torsos and necks somehow miraculously fitting together in a manner so comfortable that one is compelled to doze, dream, and smile.

But how does the spoon work, you ask? Well, it's really not that complicated. Spooning, simply, is about lying down next to someone and wrapping your arms around this other person. In essence, it's a horizontal hug. If you're still having trouble picturing this, ask a friend with a reputation as a spooner.

MISSION STATEMENT
This book has a mission:

1. To introduce those of you who've never spooned to the miracle of spooning.

2. To help those of you who do spoon take your spooning to a higher level. Consider us your spooning coaches who'll help you move from the AAA ball club of spooning to the major leagues.

3. To convince those of you who've grudgingly experienced spooning—but are skeptical of why one would willingly choose to participate in such an activity—to give it one more try.

4. To help prevent needless spooning injuries and to answer the tough questions about spooning that may be holding some back: Where do you put the extra arm? What about the dangers of overheating? What if the butts don't line up just right? How do you protect yourself from deadly hair suffocation?

5. To make spooning a household word. (Naturally!)

WHY WE SPOON

Why spoon, you may ask? Why not draw an invisible line down the bed and bid a fond farewell as you doze off? The answer is simple: spooning is one of the most intimate, warm, and fun activities that two people can share. The feeling of two bodies cocooning around each other is truly one of life's simple pleasures. Also, spooning is about survival. In the middle of winter, a good spoon may be all that stands between you and a nasty case of frostbite.

SKIN HUNGER

Spooning addresses a basic human need: skin hunger. What is skin hunger, you ask? You won't find this term in the dictionary. (Not yet. We're working on it.) Skin hunger is that feeling you get when you simply haven't been touched enough lately. Let's face it, during the day people cruise by your desk or wherever you spend your time and offer nothing but the most casual contact: an e-mail, a fax, or—if you're really lucky—a handshake. The evening comes, and your pores are hungry. You need some TLC.

Let's take pets for example. They can't talk but they definitely get their point across. You're sitting in a chair, dozing off, and they come right on up, land in your lap, and lick your face. They

We have a hypothesis. We believe that there is a direct correlation between skin hunger—and a subsequent lack of spooning—and crabbiness. We want to research this but we're having a hard time finding people willing to spoon with scientifically-selected strangers in a clinical trial.

are having skin hunger (or "fur hunger," as the case may be) and they are not afraid to ask for help.

Humans have the same need for affection but don't have a socially acceptable way to say, "Hey, touch me!" Just imagine your partner's chagrin when he finds you inching onto his lap and purring against his shoulder in a crowded restaurant. Spooning is the answer to this social dilemma. And, like our furry friends, you don't even need to speak. Just discretely roll into an available nook (make sure the nook you choose is socially correct per your surroundings) and your skin hunger will be cured in an instant. As you become bolder and more comfortable with your identity as a spooner you won't be embarrassed to say "I need the nook." A crowded restaurant still may not be the place for this show of affection, unless the Maître d' asks "Spooning or Non–Spooning?" as he escorts you to your table.

Making Yourself Spoon-Ready

**"For all the advantages of sleeping
next to another person, it's not always easy
to figure out where everything goes."**

ACTOR AND COMEDIAN PAUL REISER

Let's begin by saying that we don't want

you to think of spooning as yet another thing on your

to-do list—somewhere between "learn to play the guitar"

and "clean out the closets." Spooning isn't a new skill to

**WILL SPOONING EVER BE
  AN OLYMPIC SPORT?**
It has all the makings: an international following;
varying degrees of difficulty; emphasis on technique;
and, it's accessible to everyone. The uniforms could
even be red, white, and blue flannel pajamas (feet
optional) for the U.S. athletes. The answer so far?
We don't know. But send your petitions to the U.S.
Olympic Committee and start training.

acquire—rather it's something you have in you, like a dormant gene that needs to be awakened. In fact (almost), some of the world's top scientists are racing to find the spooning gene. We'll keep you posted. Until then, read on.

Spooning is a Zen thing. No, really, you'll see. Your mind, body, and soul become totally absorbed in one thing: the spoon. The act of spooning engages all five senses (or six, if you're that lucky). Smell the herbal essence of your partner's shampoo; enjoy the feeling of your partner's breathing; struggle to reach that itch without disturbing your partner's sleep. You'll find there are many small pleasures you never noticed before you converted to spooning.

Not to get too "Wild Kingdom" here, but spooning is kind of like the whole caterpillar-in-a-cocoon thing. Do you think a soon-to-be-butterfly is thinking of anything else (laundry, board meetings, etc.) when she's in the cocoon? Not a chance—we've polled several cocooned caterpillars on this very question. A good spoon cocoons you around your loved one so that you both emerge the next day better and brighter than before.

BACK-TO-THE-BASICS

Having said this, there are still rules to review and ideas to impart. Think of the ideas in this book as wisdom that has been passed down for generations—like an old recipe—not an ultra-modern philosophy that has anything to do with web pages or business lunches. Spooning is part of getting back to basics, the simple pleasures in life. You know, the whole Zen-simplify-your-life thing.

You say "I'm simply not a spooner. Never have been, never will be." Well, okay, we hear what you're saying. But you bought the book, did-n't you? Or someone bought it for you? Doesn't that mean that there's some itsy bitsy teeny weeny part of you that's thinking "Dang, this spooning thing may not be all bad?" Explore it. Try it. If

SETTING A SPOONFUL MOOD
What should you do to entice a skeptical partner into spooning? How can you enhance your spooning plea-sure even when both you and your partner are willing and able? The answer: set the mood. We're not talking lava lamps and track lighting. Instead, we'd like to sug-gest simple ways of turning an ordinary bedroom into "The Spoon Zone." Light a few candles. Kick back with some soothing music. Turn off the phone. Unplug the fax. Shut off the T.V. Light a little incense if that's your thing. You'll feel a spoon coming on in no time.

RELAXATION TECHNIQUE #1:
THE BATH

Bathing for two isn't just about conserving water. It's about unwinding, debriefing, and regrouping at the end of a day.

- Run the hot water.
- Add in a bubble bath of your choice.
- Submerge.
- Be aware of your partner's movements—we don't want any unnecessary bathtub injuries.
- Don't be intimidated by small tubs: simply nestle in there and breathe deeply. You'll find the concerns of the day "going down the drain" and you'll feel better prepared to spoon.

HOW TO RELAX

Spooning is completely ineffective and virtually impossible (not to mention dangerous!) if both the spooner and the spoonee are tense. Therefore, throughout the book we'll provide you with relaxation techniques that promote safe and effective spooning.

you hate it, you can go back to being a "my side, your side" kind of person. (Not that we're judging. That's not what we're about.) But if not–if it grabs you–your life will be transformed forever. Are we starting to sound like an infomercial? Read on.

THE 10 PRINCIPLES OF SPOONING

No spoon is an island. It's important to recognize that, usually, it takes two to spoon. In order for you and your partner to build a complete repertoire of effective spoons, we must first lay down—no pun intended—some ground rules. These principles should guide your spooning practice. (Sorry: we didn't mean to "should" on you, but in this case it feels appropriate. No offense intended.)

Tip: Remember that no matter how you initially position your spoon, it will inevitably change with the tides of sleep. It's kind of like synchronized swimming in bed, without the rehearsals, nose clips, brightly colored caps, exaggerated expressions, and performance pressure. So go with it, ebb and flow all night long.

1. Relax. Easier said than done.

2. Be aware of your body—limbs and all— and stretch if you feel tight. You wouldn't want to cramp up mid-spoon.

3. Remember mom's advice: always wait one-half hour after eating before attempting a spoon.

4. Visualize the spoon in your mind's eye.

5. Never force the spoon, just let it happen.

6. Always remember to breathe.

7. Keep in tune to your partner's movements and moods.

8. Strive to be the best spooner you can, but never pressure your partner.

9. Practice, practice, practice.

10. Enjoy the moment.

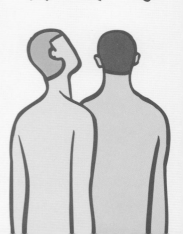

NECESSARY
EQUIPMENT

Some activities today need so much stuff. Look at hockey, for example: uniforms, pads, sticks, pucks, rink, skates, refs, bandages, and so on. Not to judge hockey. We're both big fans. But it's not just sports and hobbies that clutter our lives and garages. Our jobs and even our free time have become too complicated with faxes to send, appointments to keep, showers to take, rooms to clean, dogs to walk . . . the list is never-ending. Time to simplify. To spoon you need only a willing partner and a relatively flat surface. But to really make your spoon the best it can be, we suggest the following "equipment."

1. Clean hair. This isn't as much for you as it is for
    your partner. Wasn't it Brooke Shields who once said

she wouldn't date a smoker because it smelled up her hair? Think about it, your hair takes on all the smells of your world: smoke, smog, the pastrami sandwich with extra onions you had for lunch. Remember, when spooning, the spoonee's hair is frighteningly close to the spooner. Just a tip.

2. Plenty of pillows. The key to pillows is to have lots of them in many different sizes and levels of mushiness. As you'll see, the different spooning techniques require a variety of pillow sizes. Also, the texture of the pillowcase is important. There's nothing like feeling a soft flannel pillowcase against your face.

3. Trimmed toenails. We can't emphasize this enough! This will both prevent injuries and enhance pleasure. If trimming is an issue, don't be afraid to use socks.

Imagine there's two people
it isn't hard to see
One arm below us
above us one will be
Imagine all the people
spooning for today
You may say that I'm a dreamer
but I'm not the only one
I hope some day you'll join us
and the world will spoon as one.

POP QUIZ:
ARE YOU
SPOON-READY?

Now that you've the background necessary to become a

spooner, you probably think you're ready to jump in and

learn the techniques. As your spooning consultants, we

can't let you proceed until you've honestly evaluated your

abilities. The following test will help you determine your

spoon readiness.

Take a few moments during dinner or by the light of the fire and ask yourself and your partner these important questions. If you're in the early stages of dating with your would-be partner, you may wish to be more subtle. However, we do recommend evaluating spooning compatibility at the earliest stages of a relationship. Don't be alarmed if you're more advanced than your partner, perhaps you'll be the one to show them the way of the spoon.

Heartfelt Questions:

1. When you were a child, did you bring your teddy bear into bed with you or did you force your furry friend to sleep on a cold barren shelf?

2. Do you wake up in the middle of the night spooning your pillow?

3. Have you ever been accused of being a "bed hog" because of your encroachment upon someone else's side of the bed?

4. Do you find yourself embracing your cat for hours at a time, much to the animal's chagrin?

5. Do you find yourself attracted to the comforting heat of your sleeping partner?

6. Do you find yourself creating new spoons in the middle of an important meeting?

7. Do you think that spooning is among the top five most important things in a relationship?

8. When you go to the county fair and you see the piglets spooning, do you get all warm and fuzzy inside?

9. Have you stared down your fear of suffocating

from your partner's hair or the dreaded loss of blood flow to the arm?

10. Do you believe that spooning is the untapped key to world peace?

Scoring

If you or your partner answered yes to:

8 or more of the above questions: WOW. You're Spoon M.V.P. (Most Valuable Player). You're ready to jump feet first into even the most complex techniques and could probably create a few of your own variations.

4 to 7 of the above questions: YOU HAVE POTEN-TIAL, especially if you're a first-timer. You're Spoon-Ready. Read on and study hard.

1 to 3 of the above questions: HMMM. You're Spoon-Challenged and that's okay. You're reading this book, so we

know there's a spooner trapped inside of you. Don't worry, it's our job to cultivate this dormant spooner. Don't give up on yourself—we haven't given up on you. Review the rules and slowly read on. Proceed to the beginner spoon when you feel ready.

LET'S GET PERSONAL

We'd like to take this moment to put in a plug for including spooning prowess in personal ads. Every ad includes information about physical features, age, hobbies, and career. Why would someone leave out one of the most important aspects in any relationship: spooning compatibility. After all, how can you possibly expect to meet Mr. or Ms. Right when you aren't inquiring about their spooning abilities? An effective ad would read something like this:

I'M A SINGLE FEMALE AGE 29 WHO LIKES WALKS ON THE BEACH, ROMANTIC MOVIES, AND HEARTY SPOONS. YOU ARE A SINGLE MALE AGE 25–40 WHO HAS A GOOD SENSE OF HUMOR AND PROVIDES A GREAT NOOK. LET'S MEET AND SEE IF SPOONING IS IN OUR FUTURE.

SPOONING
BEFORE MARRIAGE

There's one topic we feel compelled to address. You may now be wondering "Do they believe in spooning before marriage?" Our answer is simple: we believe in the power of the spoon. However, everyone must make their own choice as to when they're ready to explore this power. Follow your spooning gut and you'll do the right thing. (How's that for vagueness?)

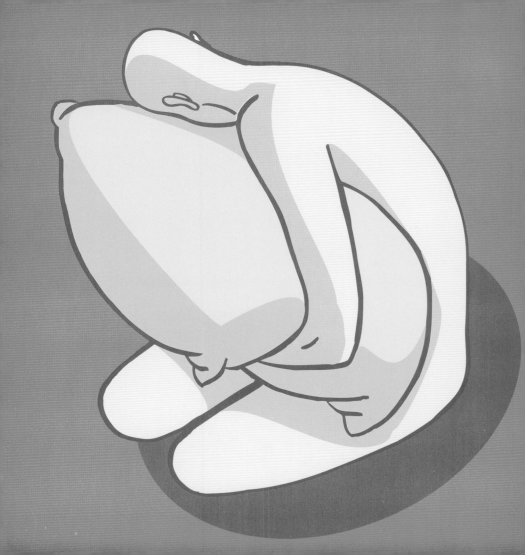

Classic Spoons and New Variations

"You're always as good as your last spoon."
ANONYMOUS 19TH–CENTURY SPOONER

Enough talk. Now it's time to put these principles into action. We'll begin with the simplest spoons and offer some techniques to get you started. For some of you this may be review—please bear with us. Our other goal in this chapter is to create a common language among spooners.

Every discipline has a shared vocabulary, why shouldn't spooning? After we've covered the beginning techniques, we'll slowly and methodically guide you through spooning variations. Don't worry, we'll be with you every step of the way. With this said, let the spooning begin!

BEGINNER TECHNIQUES
Who's Who?: Spooner & Spoonee

Throughout the techniques, we'll be referring to the "spooner" and "spoonee." To clarify, the spooner is the person who, in a standard spoon, curls up behind the spoonee so that the spooner's chest is touching the spoonee's back. In the same spoon, the spoonee is the person who is being "hugged" from behind by the spooner so that the spoonee's back is touching the spooner's chest.

Many people think that the spooner must be the taller or larger of the twosome. Untrue, this is an old wives tale (yes, old wives spooned). Though it may be easier or even more comfort-able to have the larger member be the spooner, a horizontal-ly-challenged partner can effectively initiate the spoon as well. This allows equal-opportunity spooning and— do the math—doubles the chance of a spoon happening.

RELAXATION
TECHNIQUE #2:
THE FOOT MASSAGE
Another option for decom-
pressing from the stress of
the day is the classic foot massage. Hold your partner's foot
lovingly. Cover the foot with
lotion. We recommend one with a
peppermint scent, not only will it
feel all tingly but it will help
cover up any nasty odors. Begin
by rubbing the heel, then the
arch, and finally the little pig-
gies. We need not say
more—this one is pretty
straight forward and
we swear by it.

The Standard Spoon

1. Lie down on a bed or any other flat surface. The floor or even the ground outside (for a nice picnic spoon.) will do just as nicely.

2. The spooner of the twosome takes their place behind the spoonee in a prone position.

3. Butts and hips should be in alignment. This is key!

4. The spooner places the arm closest to the bed—also known as the treacherous "under-the-body arm"—through the small tunnel made by the spoonee's neck and pillow. Without question, this dangerous maneuver is the greatest obstacle to spooning for most people. Beware! This step is tricky and not for the faint-hearted—circulation can be lost with one false move!

   Other options for the under-the-body arm

include, but are not limited to the following:

- Sliding it under your own pillow in a straight line from your shoulder toward your head.
- Curling it up like a shrimp next to your body.
- For those of you who are more limber, try sliding it behind your own back.

    Try them all to see what works best for you. Note that the size of the pillow can make a big difference here as to where and how you place your arm. Experiment with different sizes, shapes, and levels of mushiness to find what works for you.

5. The spooner's arm farthest from the bed—also known as the free "above-the-body arm"—is placed (lovingly) over the curled-up body of the spoonee.

6. Breathe deeply and enjoy. If the spoonee has long hair,

the spooner must be careful to avoid suffocation. If this happens, use the above-the-body arm to move your loved one's hair away from your windpipe. Also, lighten up—it's scientifically proven (kind of) that you can, if necessary, breathe through hair.

Congratulations—you've achieved your first spoon! This will be the bedrock of your spooning repertoire. Don't get cocky—you never outgrow the Standard Spoon, perfecting its intricacies is a lifelong learning process.

Personalizing the Standard Spoon

Though we've walked you through the general format of the Standard Spoon, don't be afraid to get creative. Consider the placement of the legs, for example. Legs can be placed close to the chest in a fetal position or stretched out and scissored around your partner.

You also can vary the Standard Spoon with the positioning of the arms. For instance, the above-the-body arm can dangle over your partner's body, hold your partner's hand, or tuck under your partner's chin. Your ability to ebb and flow with each other's movements is key to achieving successful variations. If a variation is uncomfortable, keep trying. Roll about until your spoon is completed to your satisfaction.

The Security ("You're Going Nowhere") Spoon

Are you ever concerned that if you fall asleep first, your partner will break free from the spoon and leave you to shiver alone during the night? This beginner spoon offers the simple stability of the Standard Spoon with the added assurance that your partner won't Houdini themselves to

Don't spoon angry. We can't say this enough. We believe that the angry vibes go right through the spoon, contaminating it. However, spooning can also be a therapeutic way of working through your anger. For example, your partner has done something particularly annoying that evening. You take your irritation to bed with you. Your partner brings you into the Standard Spoon and holds on until all the nasty vibes are gone. Just something to think about.

their own side of the bed.

This spoon is also particularly effective when sleeping with an early riser. For example: Let's say it's the middle of winter and your spooning partner decides to engage (foolishly) in an early morning run. You move in with a Security Spoon, your partner's plans are foiled, and you remain toasty warm.

1. Assume the Standard Spoon, taking care to be the spooner, not the spoonee.

2. The spooner takes their big toes and index toes (Is that a real term?) and "locks" them around the Achilles heel

of the spoonee. If you believe your toes are too short for this one, you're wrong. Lisa has the littlest toes ever (size 5½ shoe) and she does this like a champ. If the spooner is shorter than the spoonee, the spoonee must be in a fetal position.

SAFETY TIP: Toenail clipping becomes imperative when dealing with the Security Spoon! You can just imagine the health risks of Step 2 if it's been a while since you've used the clippers. The authors assume no liability for any lacerations or punctures associated with the improper and anti-social growing of the lower digit weaponry.

3. The spooner brings the above-the-body arm across the body and under the armpit of the spoonee. The spooner then wraps their hand around the spoonee's

wrist (gently), hence locking in the upper body. This sounds trickier than it is; don't be alarmed.

Voila. Though we don't recommend coercion be involved with your spooning, the added security never hurts.

Solo Spooning

We want to make the point here that, though spooning is one of life's greatest two-person activities, it's also something you can do alone. We totally advocate the spooning of pets—of course, only with their consent. Although, we do recommend sticking to cats and dogs and leaving your tropical fish in peace. In addition, as mentioned earlier, Lisa got her spooning start with Theodore the Bear. So stuffed animals are fair game. And, as a last resort, there's always your favorite pillow. Our point is simple: spoon, spoon, spoon. Find an opportunity and make it happen.

ADVANCED SPOONING TECHNIQUES

Now, don't be fooled—you're but an infant in the world of spooning. Many people stop here. That's okay. We're here for you. When you're ready, move on. Note: This may be a good time to review the principles and the mission statement, and maybe even retake the quiz. When you feel ready, proceed to the following techniques.

The Hair Petting ("Nook") Spoon

The Hair Petting Spoon is designed to alleviate the stress, headaches, and fears of the spoonee and to bring a sense of peace to the spooner.

1. The spooner lies on their back with their head propped up on a pillow. The spooner places a free pillow within the armpit nook. Note: the pillow provides both a

comfy cushion for the spoonee's head and a necessary shield from the day's odors.

2. The spoonee curls gently into the nook, placing their head on the pillow and lying on their back or side, depending on preference.

3. Once settled, the spooner takes the hand of their arm that is under the pillow, hooks it over the spoonee, and gently pets the forehead of the spoonee.

The Chair Spoon

The Chair Spoon provides a spoon-sensitive approach to back pain. In this position, the spoonee can experience pain relief while maintaining connection to the spooner.

1. Begin with both the spooner and the spoonee executing the Standard Spoon. Arrange your legs so that your knees are at a 90 degree angle—an L shape, for those of

you who hated high school geometry—to the hips. Let your legs dangle down from there. This will ensure that the chair does not become a chaise lounge.

2. Slowly, gingerly, and without sudden movements— it's all fun and games until someone loses an eye— the spoonee rolls onto their back toward the spooner. As you shift your position, remain aware of the position of the spooner's under-the-body arm. While executing the roll, the spoonee should envision sitting into an easy chair. Trust us, visualization does help.

   You'll know you've completed the spoon when the spoonee's legs drape over the spooner's thigh so that the thigh acts like the "seat." The spoonee's head will rest on the under-the-body arm of the spooner. This sounds more complicated than it is. Give it a try.

3. There may be a time when you wish to switch who sits in the chair and who is the chair. No problem. Gracefully, the spoonee (remember, the one sitting in the chair) rolls toward the spooner until the spoonee's legs lie on the bed with their knees at a 90 degree angle. Simultaneously, the spooner rolls onto their back, toward the spoonee, and relaxes into the chair. We don't want to throw you off but what you're doing here could result in the spooner being in the chair and the spoonee being in the nook all at once. Sound complicated? It is. If you haven't got it, don't worry—it can take years of practice. Just keep trying until you get it right.

FIGHT THE X

We feel compelled to address the bad habits of anti-spooners. One of the most blatant spooning fouls is the "X." The "X" occurs when a person, usually a non-spooner, lies in the center of the bed with their limbs extending into the four corners so they look like an X across the bed. Yes, this is comfortable for the one person involved; however, this position doesn't allow any room for spooning. None. Zip. Nada. Therefore, though it is fine to X alone, we don't recommend this behavior in tandem. Further, if you are confronted with someone who Xes, don't panic. Three offensive maneuvers we recommend:

1. An oldie, but a goodie: the ever-classic stealing of the sheets.
2. The verbal warning: "Hey, move over." This, combined with a not-too-hard elbow jab in the ribs, is always a winning move.
3. For the ardent spooner: nestling into the misbegotten nook and shimmying your way into a spoon.

"To everything there is a season and a time to every spoon under heaven."

20TH-CENTURY SPOONING ANTHEM

Spooners must adapt to changes in climate. Here are a few notes to help you modify your spoons to accommodate any variation in weather.

The Heat Wave Spoon

How many times have you heard your spooning partner say, "It's too hot to spoon." Or maybe you've said this yourself. Excuses, excuses, excuses. While the Standard Spoon is ill-equipped to serve you on summer's hottest nights, this doesn't mean that you must abandon spooning altogether. Follow these simple steps, and you'll spoon comfortably even when the mercury soars.

1. Both spooners (there is no spoonee) lie very still on their backs on their own sides of the bed.
   Note: This is the ONLY time we'll advocate for you to stay on separate sides of the bed.

2. Slowly, so as not to exert yourself in the overwhelming heat, inch the hand that is closest to your partner even closer.

3. When your hands touch, stop.

4. Take your pinkie and intertwine it with your partner's. Now your pinkies are spooning.

Variations: You may choose to do some other kind of hand-oriented spoon. For example, we aren't against the full hand hold, palm-to-palm. After all, hand holding is one of life's simple pleasures. In addition, you may choose not to involve your hands at all. Rather, you may gingerly slide one cool foot across the line to meet your partner's. Hence, a foot-to-foot spooning experience—but, remember, keep those toenails clipped!

The Sub-Zero Spoon

Our friend's grandparents, have offered a historical perspective of spooning revolving around the Sub-Zero Spoon. When these fabulous ninety-something year olds were young, the siblings would spoon together in one big bed during the cold months of the year. "Spooning was all about survival," they said.

SPOONING WHILE PREGNANT: WHAT WOULD YOUR MIDWIFE OR DOCTOR SAY?
There's currently no evidence to suggest that spooning while pregnant is harmful. In fact, we believe spooning may provide significant health benefits. Though the surgeon general has yet to support our hypothesis, we believe a statement on this subject will be forthcoming. Until then, we recommend that the pregnant party assume the spoonee position in a Standard Spoon or in a Chair Spoon.

While you may only share your bed with one other
spooner, this principle still applies. When the temperature
dips below freezing and the flannel pajamas just aren't
adequate to keep you warm, don't be afraid to cocoon into
a very tight Standard Spoon and hold on for dear life until
the morning comes. The more fetal your position the
warmer you'll be. Let your mutual body heat carry you
through the proverbial storm.

Face-to-Face Spoon

We've been having a difference of opinion as to whether

or not the Face-to-Face position is in

fact a spoon. In this position, the

spooner and the spoonee face

each other tucking their

arms in close together like

a shrimp. (Do shrimp

have arms? Well, you

get the picture.) Then,

the spooner and spoonee

simply nestle that way as

they try to figure out

what to do with

their legs.

Jim argues that this is indeed a spoon because you can still tuck and wrap legs and limbs. Lisa disagrees. She argues that it has no nooks and the bodies don't make form fitting contact as in a true spoon. Though she's a big fan of this position, she still doesn't believe it's in fact a spoon. Though Jim is willing to admit that it's less comfortable than the Standard Spoon, he feels that a spoon by any other name is still a spoon. Regardless, we both agree that breath issues became painfully obvious in this position. The jury is still out on this one.

Beyond the Bed

> **"It's our continuing mission: to seek out new spoons and to boldly spoon where no one has spooned before."**
>
> **An anonymous spooning space voyager**

As spooning zealots, we feel strongly that spooning should be a part of everyday life. With this said, we offer the following list of alternative venues where one may appropriately practice the art of spooning.

1. While in front of the fireplace:

This one speaks for itself. Sitting in front of a cozy fire provides the perfect opportunity for the Bear Hug Spoon. The spooner sits comfortably on the floor with their back propped up against a couch or an easy chair. Then, the spoonee positions themselves on the floor nestled between the spooner's legs. The spooner then wraps their arms around the spoonee gently welcoming the spoonee into a bear hug. This position enables both parties to reap the comforting benefits of the fire and, naturally, the spoon.

2. While watching T.V. or videos:

    What better time to bring your loved one into the nook than while reclining on the couch or in the big easy chair watching the tube.

3. While reading the Sunday paper:

    This requires more of a propped up spooning position. Also, it will likely include a great deal of leg wrapping as you'll need your arms free to turn the pages. The easiest way to execute this variation is for you and your partner to sit propped up on opposite sides of the couch and intertwine your legs however you find most comfortable. With your arms free, you can easily trade off sections of the paper and pass the coffee. This "legs only" spoon is an excellent way to share warmth, current events, and the funnies.

4. While camping:

This is survival spooning at its best. Whether you need comfort from the cold or soothing from your fears of bears, spooning in the great outdoors is a totally natural experience. Please note that if you're spooning aficionados like ourselves (not to toot our own horns), you may wish to invest in sleeping bags that "mate." The two bags zip together, thus allowing a full-contact spoon. Just a thought.

INAPPROPRIATE SPOONING

As we're both safety conscious people and don't want to jeopardize the public's health, we feel obligated to list some venues where spooning just wouldn't be appropriate. The following places don't lend themselves to safe, productive spooning and should be avoided when looking for a place to spoon. Note: There are no spooning safety road signs so let common sense prevail.

1. Do not spoon in a pool or other body of water, regardless of your swimming and/or spooning ability.

2. Do not spoon while driving. All it takes is one traffic accident to give spooning a bad rap.

3. Do not spoon while at a place of worship: church, temple, mosque, etc. Though we feel that spooning is sacred, there's (currently) no reference to spooning in any major religious document.

4. Do not spoon in eating establishments. This may just be a personal preference. If you find otherwise, let us know.

YOU STILL DON'T GET IT?

So, you say you're still wondering why we would ever choose to spoon? Consider it this way, we'd like you to think of spooning as a way of enhancing something you do everyday: sleeping. You have to sleep, don't you? So why not take full advantage of it and enjoy your time in bed to the fullest. Why not use the time to get closer to your partner? Why not spoon, we ask?

CAN YOU SPOON IN SPACE AND WHAT ARE THE IMPLICATIONS FOR NASA? Why haven't our tax dollars gone toward answering this question? We spend so much time trying to find life in outerspace. Well, of course there's life out there, but the more important question is do they spoon? And if they do have eight arms as reputed, where do they put them? You think we have troubles.

SPREADING THE WORD

Now that we've been through so much together—techniques, issues, creativity—we must look toward the future. As we've said before, spooning converts are often the most zealous of the bunch—like Jim, for example. For those of you paired with loving individuals who don't get the spooning thing, don't fret. Here are some helpful hints for diplomatically spreading the spoon gospel.

• Be patient. A spooner is rarely born overnight. You can't pressure someone into spooning or performance anxiety may result. (We all know how painful that can be.) Remember: you don't know if they've had a traumatic experience with spooning in the past. Maybe they choked on some hair, overheated, or their arm fell asleep.

• Be gentle. Help them talk about their negative

experiences and convince them of your sensitivity to their spooning needs. Use concrete examples of how spooning enriches your life. Utilize this book to prepare yourself to combat the most frequently used anti-spooning rhetoric: what about the arm? why bother? and all the rest. Above all, don't get self-righteous or judgmental . . . at least not at first.

IN CONCLUSION

Congratulations! Now you're a full-fledged, card-carrying spooner, entitled to all the benefits of this privilege. As fellow-spooners, we challenge you to reach new frontiers in the art of spooning. If you break new ground, we expect you to let us know (after all, we taught you everything you know). Spoon on.